Classroom Discussion Topics
Based on William Glasser's Choice Theory
and Seven Caring Versus Deadly Habits

by Dan Lukiv

First Edition: McNaughton Centre (Quesnel, BC), 2007.

Revised Edition: LukivPress (Victoria, BC), 2019.

Previously published as *The Ten Axioms, and Seven Caring Versus Deadly Habits—based on William Glasser's Choice Theory: Socio-Emotional Discussion Groups* (McNaughton Centre [Quesnel, BC], 2007).

Dan Lukiv is a poet, novelist, columnist, short story and article writer, and independent education researcher (hermeneutic phenomenology). His creative writing has appeared in 19 countries. Recently, he has been experimenting with temporal shifts and narrative strings in his haiku and senryu.

Lukiv's formal apprenticeship as a creative writer includes intensive personal direction from Canada's Professor Robert Harlow (recipient of the George Woodcock Achievement award for an outstanding literary career), the USA's Paul Bagdon (Spur Award finalist for Best Original Paperback), and England's D. M. Thomas (recipient of the Cheltenham Prize for Literature, Orwell Prize [biography], Los Angeles Fiction Prize, and Cholmondeley award for poetry), and includes studies at The University of British Columbia (The Creative Writing Department), the acclaimed Humber School for Writers (poetry writing program), and Writer's Digest School (novel writing program).

He and his wife have four daughters (married), one granddaughter, two grandsons, one step granddaughter, and one step grandson. Over many years he taught a variety of subjects (English, English Literature, communications, guitar, drama, social studies, mathematics, science, consumer education, career planning, Response Ability Pathways®, physical education, composition, and creative writing) at award-winning McNaughton Centre (Quesnel, BC), a school for troubled teenagers. Since 1978, he has edited *CHALLENGER international*, a literary journal that, over many years, focussed attention on young, up-and-coming Canadian poets, and, since 2001, he has edited *The Journal of Secondary Alternate Education*, a scholarly forum of research, practise, and theory. Through LukivPress, he has published many poetry collections, some by well-established poets such as George Swede (Canada), Paul Gotro (Canada), Elana Wolff (Canada), Bill Caughlan (Canada), Dimitar Anakiev (Slovenia), Neal Leadbeater (Scotland), Robert Lavett Smith (USA), Simon Perchik (USA), Michael J. Vaughn (USA), Esther Cameron (USA), Michael Zack (USA), Richard Luftig (USA), Luis Benitez (Argentina), and Coral Hull (Australia).

He serves as an elder in a congregation of Jehovah's Witnesses in Victoria, BC. For part of 2015, 2018, and 2019 his wife and he served together as pioneers (full-time ministers). Hobbies include longboarding, searching for haiku moments, singing and playing guitar, studying mathematics, and cycling.

Introduction

I

In this socio-emotional program, axioms are word for word quotes from Glasser's Choice Theory, and the habits come directly from Glasser's "Seven Caring Habits" and "Seven Deadly Habits."

Internet sources used:

September 13, 2007: http://www.wglasser.com/whatisct.htm

February 25, 2011: http://www.wgii.ie/static/posters/axioms.htm

January 25, 2012: http://www.wglasser.com/the-glasser-approach/choice-theory

II

Resources for discussions:

1. Students' opinions and experiences; and

2. Teacher's knowledge of Glasser's psychological theories.

III

This program should help students psychologically explore themselves and their relationships with others.

For each of 24 weeks, students construct a single class web that they daily add information to, based on the discussion topic (axiom or habit) of the week.

the discussions ... [each page affords teachers space to record the class web of the week, for future personal or professional reference]

1. Week of_____

Axiom 1: The only person whose behaviour we can control is our own. [What does that mean?]

2. Week of_____

Axiom 2: All we can give another person is information. [What does that mean?]

3. Week of_____

Axiom 3: All long-lasting psychological problems are relationship problems. [What does that mean?] [Try to think up contradictions to this "axiom."]

4. Week of_____

Axiom 4: The problem relationship is always part of our present lives. [What does that mean?]

5. Week of_____

Axiom 5: What happened in the past has everything to do with what we are today, but we can only satisfy our basic needs right now and plan to continue satisfying them in the future. [What does that mean?]

6. Week of_____

Axiom 6: We can only satisfy our needs by satisfying the pictures in our Quality World [which must address five genetic needs: survival, love and belonging, power, freedom, and fun]. [What does that mean?]

7. Week of_____

Axiom 7: All we do is behave. [What does that mean?]

8. Week of_____

Axiom 8: [All we do from birth to death is behave, and] all behaviour is Total Behaviour and is made up of four components: acting, thinking, feeling, and physiology. [What does that mean?]

9. Week of_____

Axiom 9: All Total Behavior is chosen, but we only have direct control over the acting and thinking components. We can only control our feeling and physiology indirectly through how we choose to act and think. [What does that mean?]

10. Week of_____

Axiom 10: All Total Behavior is designated by verbs and named by the part that is the most recognizable. [What does that mean?]

11. Week of_____

Seven Caring Habits: 1. Supporting. [What does that mean? Give examples that you have seen or experienced.]

12. Week of_____

Seven Caring Habits: 2. Encouraging. [What does that mean? Give examples that you have seen or experienced.]

13. Week of_____

Seven Caring Habits: 3. Listening. [What does that mean? Give examples that you have seen or experienced.]

14. Week of_____

Seven Caring Habits: 4. Accepting. [What does that mean? Give examples that you have seen or experienced.]

15. Week of_____

Seven Caring Habits: 5. Trusting. [What does that mean? Give examples that you have seen or experienced.]

16. Week of_____

Seven Caring Habits: 6. Respecting. [What does that mean? Give examples that you have seen or experienced.]

17. Week of_____

Seven Caring Habits: 7. Negotiating differences. [What does that mean? Give examples that you have seen or experienced.]

18. Week of_____

Seven Deadly Habits: 1. Criticizing. [What does that mean? Give examples that you have seen or experienced.]

19. Week of_____

Seven Deadly Habits: 2. Blaming. [What does that mean? Give examples that you have seen or experienced.]

20. Week of_____

Seven Deadly Habits: 3. Complaining. [What does that mean? Give examples that you have seen or experienced.]

21. Week of_____

Seven Deadly Habits: 4. Nagging. [What does that mean? Give examples that you have seen or experienced.]

22. Week of_____

Seven Deadly Habits: 5. Threatening. [What does that mean? Give examples that you have seen or experienced.]

23. Week of_____

Seven Deadly Habits: 6. Punishing. [What does that mean? Give examples that you have seen or experienced.]

24. Week of_____

Seven Deadly Habits: 7. Bribing or rewarding to control. [What does that mean? Give examples that you have seen or experienced.]

25. Week of_____

Let's revisit Axiom 9: All Total Behavior is chosen, but we only have direct control over the acting and thinking components. We can only control our feeling and physiology indirectly through how we choose to act and think. [What does that mean?]

the end

Made in the USA
Las Vegas, NV
30 October 2021